eyew⊙nder
Rainforest

DK

Senior Art Editor Ragini Rawat
Project Editor Upamanyu Das
Editors Zarak Rais, Shahid Qureshi
Art Editor Diya Varma
Picture Researcher Ridhima Sikka
Deputy Manager, Picture Research Virien Chopra
Managing Editor Kingshuk Ghoshal
Managing Art Editors Govind Mittal, Anna Hall
Pre-production Designer Anita Yadav
Pre-production Image Editors Vijay Kandwal, Nityanand Kumar, Rakesh Kumar
Production Editor Vishal Bhatia
Production Controller Leanne Burke
Project Jackets Art Editor Vidushi Chaudhry
DK Delhi Creative Head Malavika Talukder
Associate Publisher Gemma Farr
Art Director Mabel Chan

Consultant Dr Michael Leach

This edition published in 2025
First published in Great Britain in 2001 by
Dorling Kindersley Limited
20 Vauxhall Bridge Road,
London, SW1V 2SA

The authorised representative in the EEA is
Dorling Kindersley Verlag GmbH. Arnulfstr. 124,
80636 Munich, Germany

Copyright © 2001, 2013, 2025 Dorling Kindersley Limited
A Penguin Random House Company
10 9 8 7 6 5 4 3 2 1
001–348664–Nov/2025

All rights reserved.
No part of this publication may be reproduced, stored in or introduced into a retrieval system, or transmitted, in any form, or by any means (electronic, mechanical, photocopying, recording, or otherwise), without the prior written permission of the copyright owner.

DK values and supports copyright. Thank you for respecting intellectual property laws by not reproducing, scanning or distributing any part of this publication by any means without permission. By purchasing an authorised edition, you are supporting writers and artists and enabling DK to continue to publish books that inform and inspire readers. No part of this publication may be used or reproduced in any manner for the purpose of training artificial intelligence technologies or systems. In accordance with Article 4(3) of the DSM Directive 2019/790, DK expressly reserves this work from the text and data mining exception.

A CIP catalogue record for this book
is available from the British Library.
ISBN: 978-0-2417-3233-5

Printed and bound in China

www.dk.com

Contents

4–5
Buzzing with life

6–7
Forest layers

8–9
Amazing animals

10–11
Giant trees

12–13
Jeepers creepers

14–15
Treetop thrills

16–17
Tree houses

18–19
Life in the canopy

20–21
Forest acrobats

22–23
Happy families

24–25
The understorey

26–27
Camouflage

28–29
Lying low

30–31
Insect armies

32–33
Hunting

34–35
Riverbanks

36–37
Watery world

38–39
Night life

40–41
Temperate rainforests

42–43
Living among the trees

44–45
Exploring rainforests

46–47
Rainforests in danger

48–49
Who am I?

50–51
Ant colony

52–53
River race

54–55
Glossary and
Animal alphabet

56
Index and Acknowledgments

Buzzing with life

Monkeys call loudly from giant evergreen trees, huge spiders scuttle across your feet, and insects as big as dinner plates buzz around your ears in the rain. You're in a rainforest!

Red-and-green macaws fly over the canopy in the Amazon Rainforest.

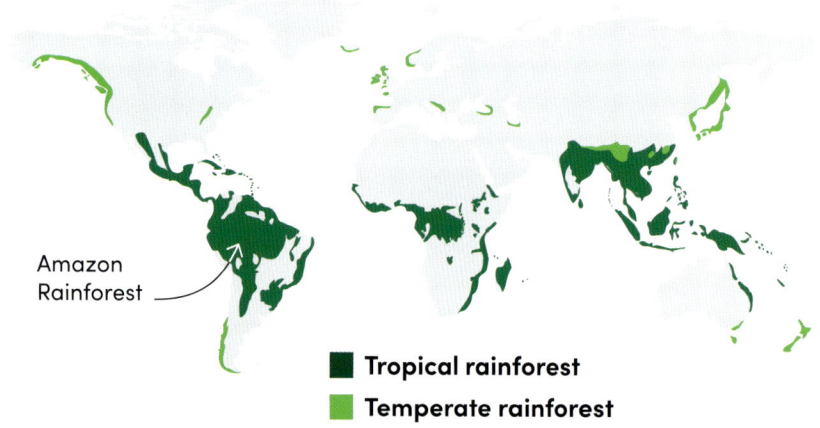

Amazon Rainforest

■ Tropical rainforest
■ Temperate rainforest

Where in the world?
There are two types of rainforests – tropical and temperate. Tropical rainforests are found in hot, damp areas. Temperate rainforests are found in cool, coastal areas.

Eastern lowland gorillas live in Africa's rainforests.

A world of animals
An incredible number of animal species – from gorillas and macaws to ants and butterflies – live in the world's rainforests.

A Queen Alexandra's birdwing butterfly rests on a leaf in an Australian rainforest.

Weather forecast
The daily weather forecast in a tropical rainforest (above) is likely to be hot and humid with heavy rain. Temperate rainforests have milder weather, with heavy rain in the winter.

Forest lifeline
The Amazon River snakes through the Amazon Rainforest, which is the world's largest. Its slow-moving waters are home to crocodiles and dolphins.

1 Emergent layer
Huge crowns of trees emerge above the forest, forming the "emergent" layer. Birds such as these hyacinth macaws love the windy conditions at the very top.

2 Canopy
The next layer – called the "canopy" – is made up of the thick branches and leaves of taller trees. A refreshing breeze and dappled sunlight make this the most popular place to live in the rainforest.

3 Understorey
Leafy bushes and small trees make up the layer above the forest floor, called the "understorey". It is dark and hot here. Hiding among the leaves are small animals as well as predators – watch out for the jaguar!

Storms and high winds lash at the treetops.

Forest layers

Each animal has its own special place in a rainforest. Its home may be located in one of the many layers of vegetation. If you start at the darkness of the forest floor, it's a long climb to the dazzling sunlight at the treetops.

4 Forest floor
The climb starts at the leafy forest floor. A soft carpet of dead leaves is a perfect habitat for clever spiders to find their next meal. Anteaters and other insect-munchers also live here.

5 Watery world
It is impossible to travel far in the rainforest without crossing one of the many streams and rivers that slice through it. Watch out for the fearsome crocs and snakes lurking in the water!

Amazing animals

A rainforest is full of multi-storey "tower blocks" of animals – with life in every layer. More than 2 million animal species live in the world's rainforests. Scientists believe there are still many more animal and plant species that we are yet to find!

Brilliant birds
Birds of every colour flash among the trees. This keel-billed toucan uses its big, colourful beak to crack open many forest fruits and nuts, attract friends, and scare away enemies.

Fast facts

Tropical rainforests receive more sunlight than temperate ones.

The Amazon Rainforest in South America covers an area equal to about 28 times the size of the UK.

A fifth of the world's bird species live in rainforests.

Mammals are animals that give birth to babies and feed them with milk.

Hopping around
This poison dart frog is among many brightly coloured frogs that you will find hopping around tropical rainforests. Frogs and toads are amphibians, which means they can live on land and in water.

Chameleons can move their eyes independently – one eye can look upwards while the other looks to the side.

Playful mammals
Tropical rainforests are the perfect playground for mammals, such as these chimpanzees, which live in Africa. They swing through the canopy in search of food, hiding from predators among the leaves.

Remarkable reptiles
Reptiles are animals with scaly skin that lay eggs. Rainforest reptiles include crocodiles, snakes, and lizards such as chameleons. This colourful panther chameleon lives in the tropical rainforests of Madagascar in Africa.

Aquatic hunter
Rivers that run through a rainforest are home to thousands of species of fish. Some eat fruits and seeds while others, such as this arapaima, are hunters.

Giant trees

The giants of the rainforest are the emergent trees which spread out above the canopy. These trees start out as tiny saplings on the forest floor and are often hundreds of years old.

Taking in the Sun
Once a young tree has grown tall enough to poke through the canopy, it spreads out its branches and enjoys the sunshine.

Starting out
When an old tree crashes to the ground, it makes a clearing. Saplings may now have the sunlight they need to grow – they race towards it, competing to take the dead tree's place.

Fast facts

Some rainforest trees may live to a ripe old age of 1,000!

Rainforest trees grow tall because they are all trying to reach sunlight.

A tree in the rainforest can have more than 50 other plant species growing on it.

Wriggly roots
Giant trees have a huge network of roots, some of which spreads out around the tree on the ground. Smaller roots wriggle across the forest floor – they draw up water and nutrients from the top, most fertile, layer of soil.

This piggyback plant from Panama's tropical rainforests has stiff, spiny leaves.

LEAFY HOMES

Tree frogs, such as this Cuban tree frog, may seek shelter among epiphytes. The leaves of some epiphytes form wells that catch rainwater like buckets. These are the perfect spots for tree frogs to lay eggs, raise their tadpoles, and keep them safe from predators.

Piggyback plants
In a rainforest, you might spot some canopy branches covered with other plants. These plants, called epiphytes, grow piggyback on the tree bark and absorb water from the air to survive.

Jeepers creepers

Rainforests are home to more than half the world's plant life. In these forests, creeper plants hang between trees and bright flowers such as orchids dot the greenery like pretty decorations.

Honeysuckle
Sweet scented honeysuckles are woody vines that scramble through the branches of temperate rainforests as they cover trees. In summer, their brightly coloured flowers are loaded with rich nectar for rainforest insects.

Wild beauty
On a walk through the Amazon Rainforest, you are likely to see a species of heliconia, also known as lobster claws. These striking flowers love the tropical heat and damp conditions of this habitat.

Tropical trap
Insects are tempted by the sweet nectar in pitcher plants. When they land on the rim, they lose their footing, fall inside, and drown in the fluid at the bottom. The plant then absorbs nutrients from them.

Spider orchid petals are long and spindly.

Blooming orchids
Colourful orchids stand out in the dense rainforest greenery. Some perch high on the branches of tall trees to absorb water from the air. Other orchids grow on the ground.

Giant flower
A Rafflesia bloom is the biggest flower in the world, but beware! It stinks of rotting meat, earning it the nickname "corpse flower". The flower opens in the dead of night in its tropical home and lasts for only one week.

The red colour of the petals looks like rotting flesh.

Treetop thrills

The animals of the emergent layer make their homes in treetops. Hidden from the forest floor, butterflies flutter in the sunshine, monkeys are chased by hungry eagles, and noisy macaws chatter about their breakfast.

Bright blue
Some flashes of bright blue seen above the Amazon treetops are the shimmering wings of morpho butterflies. Morphos are very fast and agile flyers – easy to see, but hard to catch.

Hyacinth macaws, which live in the rainforests of South America, can crack open even coconuts with their beak.

Flying nutcrackers
Macaws burst through the treetops in brightly coloured flocks. They have powerful beaks to break open even the toughest nuts.

Quick of foot
The common marmoset is a small monkey about the same size as a squirrel. Its tiny size allows it to dart among the trees of the Amazon Rainforest, catching insects, frogs, and lizards.

Shaggy crest on the head

Monkey hunter
The rare Philippine eagle is found only in the Philippines. It has broad, rounded wings to help it swoop among the branches of trees and pick off unlucky monkeys.

Marmosets gnaw at tree bark to find sap – their favourite food!

Bald head

Jungle cleaner
King vultures live in the emergent layer, but swoop down to lower levels to scavenge the remains of dead animals. Their eating habits help to keep the rainforest clean.

Ant palace
Countless ants make their homes inside the interconnected chambers of ant plants. They use these chambers like a palace, with rooms for storing food and supplies, raising their young, and even one for their queen.

Tree houses

It's bedtime in the forest, and many animals bed down in the trees. Those that step out at night will take a daytime nap, while others can't wait for a full night of sleep.

The ants collect and store plant bits, helping to provide nutrients for the ant plant.

Colugos like to hide in their holes during the day.

Hole hunt
There can be fierce competition for tree holes in the rainforest. Most animals can't make their own holes. Instead, like this colugo, they move into natural holes that form, such as when an old branch breaks away.

Spider silk is sticky, helping this green hermit hummingbird attach its nest to a leaf.

Home for dinner
Harpy eagles are one of the world's largest and strongest birds of prey. They can be seen hunting in the canopy of Central and South American rainforests. These eagles carry their prey to huge nests that can be as wide as 1.5 m (5 ft).

Cup of silk
Hermit hummingbirds are too small and delicate to make their nests out of twigs. Instead they gather spider silk with their beaks and weave it into a silken cup for their tiny chicks.

Orangutans are the largest tree-living animals in the world.

The Sumatran orangutan lives on the island of Sumatra.

Leafy bed
Did you know that an orangutan can build its nest in just a few minutes? Young apes learn how to make sleeping nests in trees by copying their parents. They bend back branches to make their bed for a comfortable night's sleep.

Fast facts

The canopy is the most densely packed layer in the rainforest.

The sunny canopy offers the most fruits, nuts, nectar, and young leaves.

Canopy leaves can be 4 m (13 ft) long – like huge, green umbrellas.

Sleepy sloths

Three-toed sloths spend their lives hanging upside down on trees. They have strong, hooked claws at the ends of their fingers, because of which they can't stand or walk easily.

An iguana stores fat under its jaws and in its neck.

Plant-like green algae often grow on the fur of these sloths, making them look green.

Gentle giant

Iguanas may look fierce, but they are timid creatures that will scamper away when scared. They are good climbers, with powerful toes and sharp claws for holding onto branches.

Life in the canopy

The dense canopy layer rings with the sound of chattering monkeys, croaking tree frogs, and hissing snakes. The thick leaves and winding branches hide friend and foe alike.

Green danger
A green tree python uses its muscular body to squeeze its prey to death. By day, it drapes itself elegantly on a branch. By night, it hunts for sleeping monkeys and birds.

The golden silk orb-weaver weaves golden-yellow webs to catch flying insects.

Canopy creatures
Many types of spiders spend their whole lives high in the canopy. This is where they feed and have babies, without ever needing to come down to the ground.

Nosy crew
Proboscis monkeys live in the canopy, where it is hard to see each other. They use sounds to communicate and find one another. The monkey's huge nose makes its call louder.

Proboscis monkeys have only one home – the rainforests on the island of Borneo.

Super swingers
Gibbons really know how to swing! This lar gibbon is speeding through the canopy in a tropical rainforest in Thailand, using its extra-long arms and legs to move from tree to tree.

Gibbons can cover a gap of 15 m (50 ft) in a single leap!

Forest acrobats

Whether they swing, jump, or glide, animals travel between trees with acrobatic style. They rarely, if ever, miss their footing and fall.

A gecko can use its tail to change direction mid-air.

Gliding geckos
These small lizards have webbed feet, and flaps of skin on their sides. When a smooth-backed gliding gecko takes off, the loose skin fills with air, letting it gently glide down.

Night flight
At night, the sugar glider takes off from a branch, its "wings" of skin billowing in the air like a parachute as it glides towards a eucalyptus tree. It is out looking for sugary sap.

Fast facts
Most canopy animals have excellent eyesight that helps them judge distances and see landing spots when leaping through branches.

Animals need to move quickly to escape predators such as hawks and eagles that hunt above the treetops.

High jumpers
Tree-kangaroos may be slow on the ground but they are fast and agile in the canopy. They can leap huge distances among the treetops – up to an astonishing 9 m (30 ft).

A twist in the tail
A spider monkey has a prehensile tail, which it uses to grasp branches like it would with a limb. This helps the animal move around quickly and pick things up.

Some brown spider monkeys have striking blue eyes.

Monkey troops

Campbell's mona monkeys live in troops of up to eight members and share friendships and family bonds. There is one ruling male in each troop, and at sunrise, he climbs on top of a tree to make loud booms.

A mona monkey's tail is longer than its body.

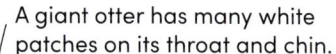
A giant otter has many white patches on its throat and chin.

Chatty clan

Giant otters live in South America. There may be up to eight members in a family group. You may find them communicating with each other using about 22 different calls – from hums to screams.

Backpacker mum
A Suriname toad mum carries her eggs under the skin on her back for up to 20 weeks! The babies hatch out as mini toads. Toads are like frogs, but with drier skin and shorter legs.

Standing guard
After a female shield bug's eggs hatch, she stands guard over her bug babies as they huddle beneath her.

Happy families

Many rainforest animals live together in organized social groups, like our families. This is how they care for each other in the wild.

Shield bug eggs are usually round and pale, translucent green.

HELPING MUM

Female primates tend to look after their young on their own, but female tamarins have some help! Male tamarins take turns to carry and raise the young, giving the mothers time to rest and stay strong.

Jungle giants
Forest elephants roam the tropical rainforests of Africa. These heavy animals live in family groups of up to 20 members.

The understorey

The plants growing in the still, hot, and humid air of the understorey of a tropical rainforest are lit with a greenish glow. Here, under the canopy, big cats slump on branches and brightly coloured birds hover around flowers.

Powerful predator

The meat-loving jaguar is the biggest cat in the Amazon Rainforest. Jaguars like to prowl the riverbanks and hook out fish with their paws. They are expert climbers.

Fast facts

The understorey is darker than the canopy because the dense leaves of the canopy stop most of the sunlight from reaching the lower parts of the rainforest.

The understorey provides shelter from the worst of the weather for small insects such as ants, bees, and beetles.

Dangerous neighbours
Lizards and frogs share the understorey with deadly animals. Snakes, such as this Amazon tree boa, lie in wait for passing prey.

Colourful chameleons
These colourful lizards can change colour. Chameleons darken to merge into their background and hide, or flash a different colour to communicate with one another.

Hungry beast
The diet of the nearly 30-cm (12-in) long Amazonian giant centipede includes insects, spiders, small birds, and bats. This venomous predator crawls about on 46 legs.

Costa Rica's violet-crowned woodnymph hummingbird feeds on nectar.

Tiny powerhouses
Hummingbirds visit thousands of flowers in a day, looking for the sugary nectar inside. This nectar gives a hummingbird energy to fly forwards and backwards, and even upside down!

Camouflage

In the rainforest, a hunter could be surrounded by prey and not know it. Suddenly, a leaf scurries away or a tree-trunk changes shape, leaving the predator stumped...

Fast facts

Camouflage is about disguise. An animal can hide by making itself seem to be something it isn't!

Camouflaged animals often look like just a dull part of their habitat, such as a mossy stone or twig.

Camouflage works best when an animal freezes or moves slowly to avoid being noticed by a predator.

Master of disguise

The leaf-tailed gecko lives in the canopy of Madagascar's tropical rainforests. When threatened by predators, it freezes and crouches close to a twig to hide its legs. This makes it look like dead leaves.

In the face of grave danger, this gecko makes sounds like a human child.

Spot the bug!
Can you see the insect in this picture? A predator is sure to overlook this false leaf katydid as it crawls on a plant. It even has spots on its body that make it seem like a caterpillar has taken a nibble.

Thorn bug
A bird would think twice before gobbling up one of these thorny insects – that's if it knew they were insects in the first place!

Hiding in the shadows
As a jaguar emerges from the shadows, the spotty markings on its coat look like the Sun shining on shady leaves. This makes it easy for the big cat to pounce on unsuspecting prey.

IN PLAIN SIGHT

Most camouflaged animals stay the same colour, but green iguanas and chameleons are different. Tiny cells in their skin move and change the way it reflects light. These animals can mirror the colour of their surroundings and blend in perfectly!

Hairy hunters
The hairy Goliath tarantula is as big as a human fist – it is one of the largest spiders in the world. It comes out of its burrow at night to hunt for food.

Fast facts

Spiders are not insects. They have eight legs, making them "arachnids".

Armadillos have 100 teeth but they hardly use them.

Gorillas are primates. A primate is a mammal that has a big brain for their body, eyes that face forwards, grasping hands, and big toes.

Lying low

Forest floor animals wind their way between trees across a carpet of dead leaves. The gloom hums with the buzz of insects, and bushes rustle as hidden predators choose their moment to pounce.

Waste nothing
Plant-like living things called fungi are great recyclers! A great example is this stinkhorn mushroom, seen on the floor of a temperate rainforest in Croatia. Fungi break down dead plants and release nutrients back into the soil to be used as food by other plants.

Armoured armadillo
A giant armadillo uses powerful claws to dig for insects and worms. Scaly armour protects its back from big cats.

Great gorillas
Gorillas live in family groups and work together to protect their territory and young. They sit on the forest floor, eating leaves as they communicate with each other using a system of grunts and body movements.

Africa's Eastern lowland gorillas are the world's largest primates.

Feathered friends
Although most birds that live on the rainforest floor can fly perfectly well, they prefer to walk and run. Flight is difficult inside a dense forest.

Green peafowl live close to water in Asia's tropical rainforests.

Insect armies

Every rainforest is alive with insects as they busily go about their daily tasks. Many live in communities that are similar to armies.

Super swarms
Each female mosquito can produce up to 200 eggs. Huge numbers of these eggs are laid in rainforest pools, where they hatch into swarms of mosquitoes.

Mosquito swarm resting on a leaf

Fast facts

Ants are the most common animals in the rainforest. More than 1,000 ant species call the Amazon Rainforest home.

Insects make up around 90 per cent of the total animal species that live in the world's rainforests.

Scientists believe they have discovered fewer than half of all insect species in our rainforests.

Tiny farmers
Leaf-cutter ants carry leaf fragments back to their underground nests. The chewed leaves make ideal compost for growing fungi – the ants' favourite food.

Leaf-cutter ants can strip a bush of all its leaves in one night.

On the rampage
At dawn, workers and soldiers from army ant communities set off to hunt, forming a long column that snakes across the forest floor. They attack and kill anything that gets in their way, even large animals.

Paper wasp nests look like upside-down umbrellas.

👁 BUILDING HOMES

Some insects work in teams to build complex, elaborate homes where they store their food, raise their young, and seek shelter. Termite mounds, ant hills, and beehives are some examples. These structures often have multiple chambers and good ventilation for air to flow.

Termite mound

Paper wasps
These little insect architects create intricate nests out of chewed wood pulp. Each nest contains rooms with eggs that hatch as wasp larvae, which will gradually turn into adult wasps.

31

Rainforest snakes may hunt by ambushing prey in the trees.

This snake can also be green or blue-green in colour.

Star striker
Poised to strike, this Indonesian pit viper waits patiently for passing prey. It will inject venom into its prey when it bites. This snake lives on Indonesia's islands and in Timor-Leste.

Clever moves
Predatory mantises sway like leaves in the breeze to fool prey. They wait patiently to launch a lightning strike on an unsuspecting prey, grabbing it with spiny forelegs.

Hunting

In the rainforest, venturing out to find food is a dangerous task – it's nothing like a trip to the supermarket! You have to be careful and lucky.

Dinnertime
When the Sun goes down, hungry vampire bats sneak up on mammals and birds, gently bite into their skin, and lick blood from the wound.

Night vision
While hunting at night, this western tarsier has caught a snack – a crunchy cicada. It's thanks to its big eyes that it can see well in the dark.

This tarsier can be found in the tropical rainforests of Borneo and Sumatra in Southeast Asia.

Dark patches on its legs help this spider blend in with the forest floor.

On the hunt
Brazilian wandering spiders do not build webs. They roam the forest floor, searching for insects, small reptiles, and even mice to eat.

Riverbanks

Rainforest riverbanks are alive with wildlife. Gentle plant-eaters browse the thick vegetation, graceful birds show off their fishing skills, and giant snakes lie in wait for passing prey...

Walking on water
The basilisk lizard has webbed toes on its hind feet, which help it dash across the water's surface quickly to escape danger.

Egrets use their sharp beaks to spear small prey.

Snappy beaks
Peru's elegant great white egrets patiently stalk the river, snapping up fish, frogs, and insects. At dusk, they return to nearby trees to roost.

A tight squeeze

Anacondas – the biggest snakes in the world – can be as long as a school bus. One of the few predators of adult crocodiles, an anaconda will squeeze a croc to death, then eat it whole.

Green anacondas are found only in South America's tropical rainforests.

A tapir's long nose acts as a snorkel, helping it breathe underwater.

Timid tapirs

A Brazilian tapir would make a tasty meal for many big predators. But this gentle plant-eater is an excellent swimmer and can stay underwater for a few minutes if it needs to hide from a hungry jaguar.

Fast facts

Riverbank animals can find food in both the water and forest.

Capybaras are the biggest rodents in the world. They are the same size as pigs.

Female anacondas are five times longer than the males. They can grow as long as 8 m (26 ft)!

Lazy swimmers

The rodents called capybaras are good swimmers thanks to their partially webbed feet. Often seen floating in some South American rivers, they like to sleep in the water with just their noses above it.

Largest leaves

In the rainforest, aquatic plants thrive where rivers are slow-moving, shallow, and swampy. Amazon water lilies grow in parts of the Amazon Rainforest. They have the largest leaves among all plants.

Bulls-eye!

Archerfish are skilled shooters – they can spit water at insects as far as 1.5 m (5 ft) above the surface and score a direct hit. This knocks the insect into the water, where the archerfish gobbles it up.

Hungry dolphins

Amazon river dolphins are grey at birth and turn pink as they get older. They eat more kinds of fish than any other dolphin, even gobbling up scary piranhas.

Yacare caimans hunt in the rivers and lakes of South America's rainforests.

Lethal jaws

Not many predators can match the ferocity of a type of crocodile called a caiman. It lunges at its prey, grabs its victim with its jaws, and spins round to tear off bite-sized chunks.

Amazon water lilies grow quickly, forming floating rafts on the river.

Watery world

A rainforest river may look calm from above, but not all is quiet underneath the water's surface. Shoals of fish and pods of dolphins dart about, sometimes on the run from ferocious hunters.

Large nasal pits help piranhas smell blood in the water up to 3.2 km (2 miles) away.

Deadly swarm
Don't be fooled by this quietly moving school of red-bellied piranhas – it can tear a large animal to pieces in minutes. When eating prey, these fish may even take bites out of each other!

Star chomper
All piranhas have sharp teeth, but South America's red-bellied piranha has sharper teeth than the rest. It can even bite through bone!

Prowling predators

Tigers are nocturnal hunters that prowl the rainforest looking for food. In the dark, they can see six times better than a human, making it easy for them to catch prey hiding in the forest's depths.

Sumatran tigers are found only on the island of Sumatra, Indonesia.

Night fishing

Fishing bats don't need to see well as they have amazing hearing. They can find fish in the river just by sensing the ripples on the surface. They hook fish out with their claws, then kill them with their teeth.

Fast facts

Owl butterflies are as big as dinner plates, with wingspans as large as 20 cm (8 in).

A tiger's roar can be heard 2.5 km (1.5 miles) away – that's very loud indeed!

Bats can't see well in the dark. They make sounds and then find their way by listening for echoes returning from their surroundings.

The yellow and black spots are visible while the owl butterfly is resting.

Spot the difference
The spots on an owl butterfly's wings might look like the eyes of an owl to a nocturnal predator in South America's rainforests. Many small animals prefer to avoid owls.

Grubby meals
The long-fingered aye-aye is the world's largest nocturnal primate. It has a hooked nail on its thin third finger, which comes in handy when digging out grubs (insect larvae) from tree holes.

Night life

For many rainforest creatures, the Sun going down is an alarm clock to get up. Animals that wake up at night are called "nocturnal". They have special features that help them hunt and survive in the dark.

A spotted cuscus spends its entire life in a tree.

Hide and seek
Australia's common spotted cuscus sleeps all day and feeds on plants at night. This shy creature prefers to hide from predators in tree holes and among leaves.

The animal grips branches firmly with its bald tail.

Fruitful forests
Some temperate rainforests, such as the Hoh Rainforest in the US, have trees that drop their leaves in the autumn. Their nuts and berries ripen in the autumn too, providing plenty of food for the local wildlife.

Moss covers most trees in temperate rainforests.

Forest snow
Winter can bring deep drifts of snow to temperate forests. It can last for months, making food much harder to find than in the bountiful summer and autumn months.

A black bear can sleep for up to six months.

Super snooze
Animals meet the challenges of changing seasons in different ways. Some store food, some migrate to warmer places, and others hibernate – they eat as much as they can in the autumn, sleep through the winter, and wake up in the spring.

Fantastic fungi
Some of the world's most beautiful and dangerous fungi grow in temperate rainforests. These fly agaric mushrooms (left) are poisonous to eat.

Temperate rainforests

Unlike hot and wet tropical rainforests, temperate rainforests have seasons, and all the ups and downs that come with them. Animals that live here must learn to survive in hot, warm, cold, and even freezing conditions.

Sun seekers
Many birds leave the temperate rainforests before snow arrives. Yellow warblers spend summers in the rainforests of Alaska, US, but fly to warmer South America to escape the chilly winter.

Living among the trees

It's not just animals that live in rainforests – people live here too. Some people spend their whole lives in these forests, living in communities and getting what they need from the plants and animals around them.

A Baka hunter sets up an animal trap made from forest vines in the rainforests of the Central African Republic.

Finding food
Hunting is an important part of finding food in the rainforest. Some people only take what they need, so that their hunting does not harm the forest.

Forest village
Some Indigenous people build large community homes. The Yanomami people of the Amazon Rainforest live in large shared shabonos, which are cleared areas of forest with a long roof around the edge.

The sloped roof offers shade from the heat of the day.

Getting around

The fastest way to travel through dense undergrowth is often on water. Rafts and boats, such as this one used by the Yanomami, let people glide through the rainforest without having to clear a path.

Boats are often made from hollowed-out logs.

Protecting the forest

In some places, people protect the rainforest against poachers and loggers. This Tembé warrior guards his people's lands in the Amazon Rainforest.

 FORESTS UNDER THREAT

Some groups of people in the rainforest have lived there for many generations. Many of them are speaking out about the damage that mining and logging is doing to their homes. In 2021, the Waorani people of Ecuador protested against government plans that would allow new oil mining on their lands.

Wild yams can bring relief to patients with pain in the body's joints.

Exploring rainforests

From tasty treats such as chocolate to plants that could help us cure diseases, rainforests have a lot to give us. Scientists explore forest layers, study wildlife, and find new species every day, but there are still many secrets left to discover!

Finding a cure

A quarter of all modern medicines come from rainforest plants. The more we study the rainforests, the more likely it is that we will find cures for many diseases.

Achiote seeds in pod

On your plate

Chocolate, bananas, and pineapples were all first found in rainforests. An orange-red food colouring called annatto is used in cheese and savoury snacks. It comes from the seeds of the achiote tree, which is found in the rainforests of Central and South America.

Study time

Scientists go deep into the rainforest to try and document all the different plants and animals they see. This scientist (left) is pointing at epiphytes in a rainforest in western India.

An ocelot looks curiously into a trail camera in a rainforest in Costa Rica.

Watching wildlife

New technologies help us learn more about rainforest animals. Tools such as trail cameras, which are mounted on trees, help us study these animals in their natural habitat.

New heights

Some scientists explore the rainforest canopy after climbing with the help of pulleys and ropes or by using walkways (right). Up there, in the forest roof, they might find animals and plants no one has ever seen before!

Deforestation

Rainforests are threatened by deforestation. This is the cutting down of trees on a large scale – for wood, farmland, or industry.

Mining

Deep inside some rainforests are mines that extract diamonds, gold, and even oil. They destroy huge areas of forest and pollute the water.

Rainforests in danger

Rainforests are shrinking, because humans are cutting down trees. This harms the habitat and the wildlife and people living in it. But scientists and local communities are working to protect the rainforests and restore them.

Homes destroyed

When trees are cut down, animals lose their homes. Without safe places to live, animals cannot survive. Some of them have now completely died out. Mining and logging also damage the homes of Indigenous peoples.

Home again
Scientists look after some endangered animals in protected spaces. Once there are enough of them, the animals can be released back into a suitable protected rainforest, where their numbers may rise.

Orangutans with carers in a rainforest in Borneo, Indonesia

Protected places
Some parts of the rainforest have been turned into wildlife reserves where people cannot hunt. Rare and endangered species, such as this three-toed sloth, can live here safely.

Planting forests
Many people are now working to plant new rainforests in areas where the original forest was cut down. Young plants are often grown in nurseries, before they are ready to be planted.

Who am I?

Take a look at these close ups of plants and animals in the book, and see if you can identify them. The clues will help.

1
- I can change my skin colour.
- I can look in two directions at the same time.

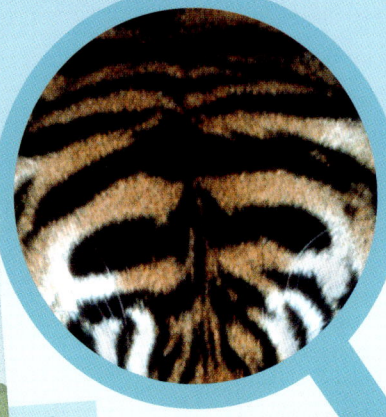

2
- I prowl the forest at night looking for prey.
- In the dark, my eyesight is six times better than a human.

3
- I have big furry ears.
- I am the size of a squirrel.
- I eat insects, frogs, and small lizards.

4
- I have a very powerful beak.
- I can crack open tough nuts.

5
- I hang upside down on trees.
- I may look green from the algae growing on my fur.

6
- In the plant world, I have the largest leaves of all.
- My leaves form floating rafts on the water.

7
- I swim in the waters of the Amazon River.
- My skin turns pink as I grow older.

8
- I am the biggest flower in the world.
- I smell like rotting meat.

9
- My wings have spots that look like an owl's eye.
- My markings may fool predators.

10
- I am a type of crocodile.
- I grab prey with my jaws and spin round to tear off its flesh.

Answers: 1.Chameleon 2.Tiger 3.Common marmoset 4.Hyacinth macaw 5.Three-toed sloth 6.Amazon water lily 7.Amazon river dolphin 8.Rafflesia 9.Owl butterfly 10.Caiman

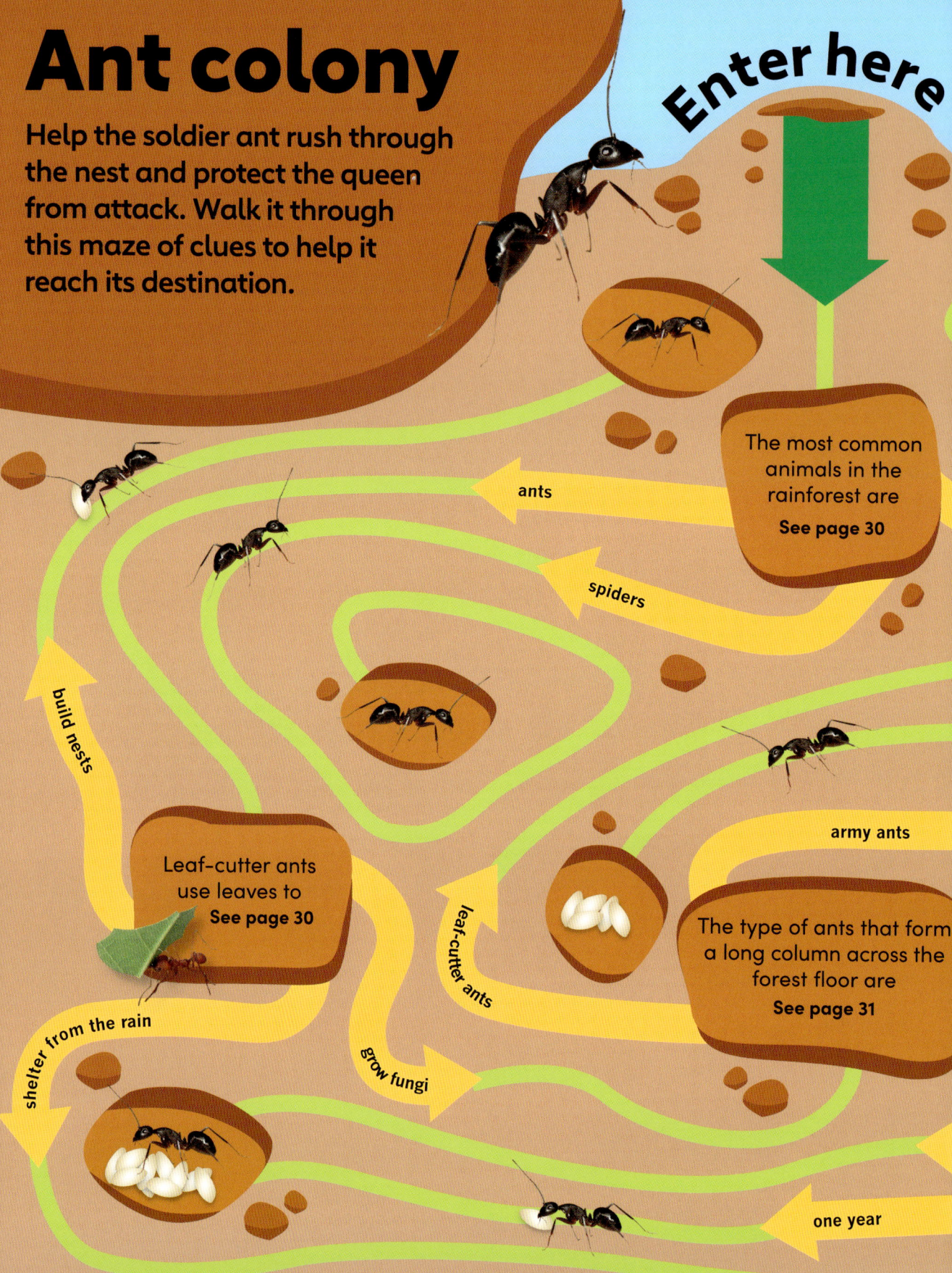

River race

A scientist has lost her way in the Amazon Rainforest. Can you help her reach the safety of her camp? A few friendly animals are ready to help!

How to play

This is a game for up to four players. You will need a dice and counters for each player. You could use counters from other board games you might have, or you could make your own counters with coloured paper – one colour for each player.

Each player takes turns to throw the dice, and begins from the START box. Follow the squares with each roll of the dice. If you land on an instruction, make sure you do as it says. Good luck!

→ **Move back!**

← **Move ahead!**

Start

You missed the owl butterfly hiding in the trees – it is hidden too well. **Miss a turn.**

An orangutan peeps through the thick leafy cover to give you company. **Move three spaces.**

A school of piranhas is hungry and ready to attack you. **Jump back five spaces.**

Glossary

Algae Plant-like, usually water-dwelling organisms with no stems or leaves.

Amphibian An animal that can live in and out of water.

Armour A hard covering that protects the body from damage.

Bloom Produce flowers.

Camouflage A colour or pattern that matches an animal's surroundings and helps disguise it.

Echo A sound caused by sound waves reflecting off a surface and back to the listener.

Epiphyte A plant that grows "piggyback" on another plant, without stealing water or nutrients from it.

Evergreen A plant that keeps its leaves all year long.

Fertile (soil) Rich in nutrients, where plants can grow more easily.

Grubs The worm-like larvae of certain insects.

Habitat The natural home of a plant or animal, such as a forest or meadow.

Indigenous The original inhabitants of a land or country.

Insect An animal with three parts to its body and six legs, such as a fly or ant.

Mammal An animal that has hair and feeds its young with milk.

Nectar The sweet liquid inside flowers.

Nocturnal Active at night.

Nutrients The food that a living thing needs to grow and live healthily.

Omnivore An animal that eats plants and meat.

Predator An animal that hunts other animals for food.

Prehensile tail A tail that can grasp (like a hand).

Prey An animal hunted for food.

Raft A floating structure made of wood fastened together.

Reptile An animal that has scales and lays eggs.

Rodent A mammal that has long, sharp front teeth, like a squirrel.

Roost To rest or sleep, often in a tree.

Sapling A young tree.

Swarm A large number of flying insects, flying closely together in a group.

Temperate Somewhere with a climate that is neither extremely hot nor extremely cold.

Translucent A substance that is almost see-through.

Tropical Somewhere with a climate that is often hot and humid.

Vegetation Plant matter.

Venomous An animal that is able to secrete a toxic substance called venom, often used in an attack.

Wingspan The distance from wing-tip to wing-tip.

Animal alphabet

Every animal pictured in this book is listed here in alphabetical order. Use the page numbers to find them.

African forest elephant 23
The smallest elephant species.

Amazon river dolphin 36
A pink-coloured mammal with sensitive hairs on its nose, which let it feel for food in dark muddy rivers.

Amazon tree boa 25
A tree-living snake that strangles prey to kill it.

Amazonian giant centipede 25
The world's largest centipede.

Arapaima 9
A meat-eating freshwater fish that has been around for 25 million years.

Archerfish 36
A fish that spits water into the air to push its prey into the water.

Army ant 30-31
A predatory ant that lives in colonies of half a million, and can kill and eat any small animal it encounters.

Aye-aye 39
A nocturnal lemur that uses its long third finger to probe for insects.

Black bear 40
A large bear that eats grass, nuts, insects, fruit, and carrion.

Blue morpho butterfly 14
A butterfly that feeds on over-ripe fruit on the forest floor.

Borneo orangutan 46, 47
An orangutan from Borneo, Indonesia. Orangutans are the largest tree-climbing animals.

Brazilian tapir 35
A ground-dwelling mammal, which uses its sharp teeth to defend itself.

Brazilian wandering spider 33
One of the world's most dangerous spiders, with a highly venomous bite.

Brown spider monkey 21
A monkey known for its prehensile tail and unusual light blue eyes.

Campbell's mona monkey 22
A monkey that uses different calls to signal distress, danger, and hunger.

Capybara 35
The world's largest rodent.

Chimpanzee 9
A primate that is the closest animal relative to humans.

Colugo 16
A flying lemur that can spread its limbs and glide between trees.

Common marmoset 15
A primate that lives in family groups of around ten members.

Common spotted cuscus 39
A tree-dwelling mammal that marks territory by licking branches, leaving a strong smell that warns away rivals.

Common vampire bat 33
A small bat that drinks blood, mainly from livestock, such as cows.

Cuban tree frog 11
A large tree frog that eats insects and spiders, as well as other frogs, toads, and lizards.

Eastern lowland gorilla 5, 29
A large primate that lives in family groups. Old males with grey hair are known as silverbacks.

False leaf katydid 27
A bush cricket. Males make chirping noises to attract mates, by rubbing their wings together.

Geoffroy's tamarin 23
One of the smallest primates in the world, weighing less than 500 g (1.1 lb).

Giant otter 22
A large meat-eating otter that can run and swim fast.

Great white egret 34
A large heron that uses its dagger-like bill to fish for food.

Greater bulldog bat 38
A fishing bat that roosts in groups in caves or hollow trees near water.

Green anaconda 35
A large, heavy snake that lives in rivers and swamps in South America.

Giant armadillo 28
A large mammal with a protective covering made of bony plates and tough skin.

Green basilisk 34
A lizard that can move quickly across the surface of water.

Green hermit hummingbird 17
A large hummingbird, which drinks nectar from flowers.

Green peafowl 29
A ground-living bird. Males spread their large tails into fans to impress females.

Green tree python 19
A slim, bright green snake that hunts mammals and reptiles in the trees.

Golden silk orb-weaver 19
A spider that produces golden silk. Its webs can reach 2 m (78 in) wide.

Goliath tarantula 28
The world's biggest spider.

Harpy eagle 17
A large eagle with eyesight eight times sharper than a human's.

Howler monkey 6
A monkey famous for its screaming morning howls.

Hyacinth macaw 6, 14
The world's largest flying macaw, very rarely spotted in the wild.

Iguana 18, 27
A plant-eating reptile with long, sharp claws, which it uses for climbing trees to feed.

Indonesian pit viper 32
A snake with a venomous bite. The toxic venom weakens the prey before the viper swallows it whole.

Jaguar 6, 24, 27, 54
A big cat and top predator, which has flower-shaped black spots called rosettes on its orange fur.

Keel-billed toucan 8
A small bird with a large, yet light beak made of hollow bone.

King vulture 15
A bald-headed vulture that feeds on prey that is already dead.

Lar gibbon 20
A small primate with soft fur and no tail. It lives high up in the tree canopy.

Leaf-cutter ant 30, 31
An ant that cuts pieces of leaves to carry back to its nest. Each nest has around 2,000 chambers.

Leaf-tailed gecko 26
A lizard with a leaf-like body and tail, which help it disguise itself among its leafy surroundings.

Mosquito 30
A small insect that feeds on plant nectar or animal blood.

Ocelot 45
A small cat that lives close to water and is an expert swimmer.

Owl butterfly 39
A butterfly that prefers to fly at dusk when fewer predators are hunting.

Paper wasp 31
A wasp that makes paper nests by chewing plant fibres.

Panther chameleon 9
A lizard with a tongue longer than its body. It can snatch insects without moving position.

Philippine eagle 15
An eagle with a diet that includes birds, reptiles, and mammals.

Pinktoe tarantula 7
A large night-hunting spider.

Poison dart frog 8
A highly poisonous, jewel-like frog that comes in many colours.

Proboscis monkey 19
A long-nosed monkey. The nose of a male continues to grow over its lifetime.

Queen Alexandra's birdwing 5
The world's largest butterfly, with a wingspan of up to 28 cm (11 in).

Red-and-green macaw 4, 5
A brightly coloured parrot that flies through the rainforest in large flocks.

Red-bellied piranha 37
A sharp-toothed, meat-eating fish that eats shrimp and molluscs.

Shield bug 23
A triangular-shaped insect, which uses its bright colours to warn predators of its horrible taste.

Smooth-backed gliding gecko 21
A lizard with sticky pads on its toes to help it climb trees.

Spectacled caiman 7
A type of crocodile called a caiman, which has a bony ridge above its eyes that look like reading glasses.

Sugar glider 21
A small mammal that eats sugary flower nectar and sticky, sweet tree sap.

Sumatran tiger 38
A type of tiger. It is the most powerful predator on the island of Sumatra, Indonesia.

Sumatran orangutan 17
An endangered orangutan that lives on the island of Sumatra.

Suriname toad 23
A flat-bodied toad. Females keep eggs under the skin of their back.

Thorn bug 27
An insect with a body shaped like a thorn, which lets it disguise itself.

Three-toed sloth 18, 47
A slow-moving sloth with three toes on each foot. It spends a lot of time hanging upside-down from branches.

Tree-kangaroo 21
A type of kangaroo, which is an agile climber.

Tropical shield mantis 32
A lightning-fast predatory insect that eats prey as large as hummingbirds.

Violet-crowned woodnymph 25
A type of hummingbird that has violet-coloured feathers on its head.

Western tarsier 33
A big-eyed primate. Each of its eyes is larger than its brain.

Yacare caiman 36
A medium-sized caiman that lives in the rivers of South America.

Yellow warbler 41
A small, brightly coloured songbird, which flies an average of 16,000 km (10,000 miles) a year.

Index

AB
achiote trees 44
anacondas 35
ants 16, 30–31
aquatic life 7, 9, 36–37
archerfish 36
armadillos 28
aye-ayes 39
bats 33, 38
berries 40
birds 4, 6, 8, 15, 17, 25, 29, 34, 41
boas 25
boats 43
bugs 23, 27
butterflies 5, 14, 39

CDE
camouflage 26–27
canopy layer 6, 10, 18–19, 21
capybaras 35
centipedes 25
chameleons 9, 25, 27
colugos 16
conservation 47
crocodiles 7, 36
cuscuses 39
deforestation 46
dolphins 36
eagles 15, 17
egrets 34
elephants 23
emergent layer 6, 14–15
epiphytes 11, 44

FGH
family groups 22–23, 29
flowers 12–13, 25
forest floor 7, 11, 28–29, 33
frogs 8, 11
fungi 28, 41
geckos 20, 26
gibbons 20
gorillas 5, 29
heliconias 12
hibernation 40
honeysuckles 12
houses 16–17, 31, 42, 46
hummingbirds 17, 25

IJKL
iguanas 18, 27
Indigenous peoples 42–43
jaguars 24, 27
katydids 27
layers, forest 6–7
leaves 30, 36, 40
lizards 20, 25, 34
logging 43, 46

MNO
macaws 4, 14
mantises 32
marmosets 15
medicines 44
mining 43, 46
mona monkeys 22
monkeys 15, 19, 21, 22, 23
mosquitoes 30
mushrooms 28, 41
nests 17, 31
nocturnal animals 38–39
ocelots 45
orangutans 17, 47
orchids 13
otters 22

PRS
peafowl 29
people 42–43, 47
piranhas 37
pitcher plants 12
poaching 43
proboscis monkeys 19
pythons 18
rafflesias 13
riverbanks 34–35
rivers 5, 7, 35, 36–37
rodents 35
roots 11
saplings 10
scientific research 44–45
sloths 18, 47
snakes 19, 25, 32, 35
spider monkeys 21
spiders 19, 28, 33
sugar gliders 21

T
tamarins
tapirs 35
tarantulas 28
tarsiers 33
temperate rainforests 4, 5, 40–41
tigers 38
toads 8, 23
toucans 8
tree-kangaroos 21
trees 10–11, 16–17, 46
tropical rainforests 4, 5

UVW
understorey layer 6, 24–25
villages 42
vipers 32
vultures 15
wasps 31
water lilies 36–37
weather 5
wildlife reserves 47

Acknowledgments

DK would like to thank the following people for their help with making the book: Lizzie Munsey for text contributions; Vandana Likhmania for editorial assistance; Revati Anand for design assistance; Samrajkumar S for picture research administration; Manu Shadow Velasco and the DK Diversity & Inclusion team for sensitivity reading; Caroline Stamps for proofreading; and Elizabeth Wise for indexing.

The publisher would like to thank the following for their kind permission to reproduce their photographs:
(Key: a-above; b-below/bottom; c-centre; f-far; l-left; r-right; t-top)

1 Alamy Stock Photo: Minden Pictures / Glenn Bartley / BIA. **2 naturepl.com:** Maxime Aliaga (br). **3 Alamy Stock Photo:** imageBROKER.com / Marko Von Der Osten (tr). **naturepl.com:** Christophe Courteau (br); Michael & Patricia Fogden (tl). **4-5 Science Photo Library:** Nature Picture Library / Nick Garbutt (t). **5 Alamy Stock Photo:** Mauritius Images GmbH / Reinhard Eisele (crb); Steve Bloom Images / Nick Garbutt (b). **Dreamstime.com:** Simon Eeman (tr); Wouter Tolenaars (c). **6 Getty Images:** 500px / Fauzan Hilmy (bc). **Getty Images:** Davehudsonphotography (c); Tarcisio Schnaider (tc). **7 Dreamstime.com:** Steven Prorak (tc). **Shutterstock.com:** Sputnik 360 (bc). **8-9 naturepl.com:** Guy Edwardes (t). **8 Alamy Stock Photo:** Daniel Borzynski (tl). **9 Alamy Stock Photo:** Nature Picture Library / Marko Von Der Osten (c). **naturepl.com:** Brandon Cole (bl); Suzi Eszterhas (tr); Edwin Giesbers (cla). **10 Alamy Stock Photo:** Steve Taylor ARPS (crb). **Dreamstime.com:** Ivan Kokoulin (l). **11 Dreamstime.com:** Gzstudio77 (tl); Markpittimages (bl). **Getty Images:** Moment / Zen Rial (cr). **12 Alamy Stock Photo:** Minden Pictures / Thomas Marent (br); Southeast Asia (b); Universal Images Group North America LLC / DeAgostini Picture Library (c). **Getty Images / iStock:** PicturePartners (tr). **13 Dreamstime.com:** Khairil Azhar Junos (tc). **14 Alamy Stock Photo:** Nature Picture Library / Bence Mate (br). **naturepl.com:** Michael & Patricia Fogden (tr). **15 Adobe Stock:** Adammajor (bl). **Alamy Stock Photo:** Nature Picture Library / Bence Mate (br). **naturepl.com:** Klaus Nigge (cla). **16 Alamy Stock Photo:** Media Drum World (br). **16-17 naturepl.com:** Maxime Aliaga (b). **17 Alamy Stock Photo:** Minden Pictures / Michael & Patricia Fogden (tr); Nature Picture Library / Hermann Brehm (tl). **18 Getty Images:** Moment / Zen Rial (crb); Moment / © Juan Carlos Vindas (br). **19 Alamy Stock Photo:** imageBROKER.com / Moritz Wolf (cl). **Dreamstime.com:** Dwiputra18 (tr). **Getty Images / iStock:** E+ / Miskani (br). **20-21 Getty Images / iStock:** Kuntalee Rangnoi (t). **20 Ardea:** Jean Paul Ferrero (br). **21 Alamy Stock Photo:** Gabbro (br); Nature Picture Library / Jurgen Freund (cla). **22-23 Alamy Stock Photo:** Friedrich Stark (t). **22 Getty Images / iStock:** Mlharing (tl). **23 Alamy Stock Photo:** Biosphoto / Vincent Premel (tc). Biosphoto / Ignacio Yufera (bl). **Dreamstime.com:** Sergey Uryadnikov (br). **Getty Images:** Moment Open / Chris Minihane (cra). **24 Alamy Stock Photo:** Octavio Campos Salles (b). **24-25 Dreamstime.com:** Amwu (tc); Dirk Ercken (tc/Background). **25 Alamy Stock Photo:** imageBROKER / Marko von der Osten (cl); Minden Pictures / Glenn Bartley / BIA (br). **Shutterstock.com:** Skifbook (cra). **26-27 naturepl.com:** Thomas Marent (b). **27 Alamy Stock Photo:** Martin Shields (tr). **Getty Images:** Moment / Sergio Amiti (br); Stone / Jami Tarris (clb). **Shutterstock.com:** PeingjaiChiangmai (tl). **28 Getty Images:** Moment / Sanja Baljkas (cra); The Image Bank / Kevin Schafer (bl). **Shutterstock.com:** Reptiles4all (tl). **28-29 naturepl.com:** Christophe Courteau (t). **29 Getty Images:** Moment / Chuchart Duangdaw (bl). **30 Alamy Stock Photo:** imageBROKER / Jürgen & Christine Sohns (br). **Getty Images / iStock:** Dmitry_7 (cla). **30-31 naturepl.com:** Konrad Wothe (tc). **31 Alamy Stock Photo:** Arterra Picture Library / Clement Philippe (tr); imageBROKER.com

GmbH & Co. KG / Arco / TUNS (b). **naturepl.com:** Jabruson (clb). **32 Alamy Stock Photo:** Nature Picture Library / Lucas Bustamante (bc); Room The Agency / Kuritafsheen (t). **33 Alamy Stock Photo:** Blickwinkel / G. Kunz (br); Nature Picture Library / Nick Hawkins (tr). **Getty Images:** Universal Images Group / Auscape (cl). **34-35 naturepl.com:** Maxime Aliaga (b). **35 123RF.com:** Raysnapper64 (br). **Alamy Stock Photo:** Biosphoto / Vincent Premel (tr); David Plummer (cla). **36 Adobe Stock:** Staffan Widstrand (b). **Alamy Stock Photo:** Avalon.red / Stephen Dalton (cla). **Getty Images:** Moment Mobile / Schafer & Hill (cra). **36-37 Getty Images / iStock:** Wika1979 (t). **37 Alamy Stock Photo:** imageBROKER.com / Sohns (bc). **Depositphotos Inc:** Robball (clb). **38 Alamy Stock Photo:** Joe Blossom (l). **naturepl.com:** Christian Ziegler (cra). **38-39 Alamy Stock Photo:** Morley Read (tc). **39 Ardea:** © Jean-Paul Ferrero (br). **naturepl.com:** Nick Garbutt (tr). **40-41 Alamy Stock Photo:** Jamie Pham (t). **40 Alamy Stock Photo:** Minden Pictures / Mark Raycroft (cb). **Getty Images / iStock:** 4nadia (bl). **41 Adobe Stock:** FotoRequest (tl). **naturepl.com:** Nick Garbutt (c). **42 Alamy Stock Photo:** imageBROKER / Fabian von Poser (cl); Robertharding / Michael Runkel (br). **42-43 Alamy Stock Photo:** Robertharding / Michael Runkel (t). **43 Alamy Stock Photo:** Associated Press / Luis Andres Henao (cb); DPA Picture Alliance / Juan Diego Montenegro (br). **44 Dreamstime.com:** Boonchuay Iamsumang (tl); Rodrigo De Souza Mendes Junqueira (c). **Getty Images:** AFP / Manjunath Kiran (bl). **45 Alamy Stock Photo:** Nature Picture Library / Nick Hawkins (tc); Nature Picture Library / Pete Oxford (r). **Getty Images:** LightRocket / Jonas Gratzer (cla). **46 Dreamstime.com:** Andrii Biletskyi (cla). **Getty Images:** Ulet Ifansasti (bl). **46-47 Alamy Stock Photo:** Nature Picture Library / Florian Kopp (b). **Getty Images:** AFP / Evaristo SA (tc). **47 Alamy Stock Photo:** Adam Major (cl); Nature Picture Library / Mark MacEwen (tr). **48 Alamy Stock Photo:** Joe Blossom (ca); imageBROKER.com / Marko Von Der Osten (cla); Nature Picture Library / Ben Cranke (cra); Nature Picture Library / Bence Mate (cb). **Getty Images:** Moment / © Juan Carlos Vindas (crb). **49 Adobe Stock:** Staffan Widstrand (crb). **Alamy Stock Photo:** Morley Read (cb); Southeast Asia (clb). **Getty Images:** Moment Mobile / Schafer & Hill (tc). **Getty Images / iStock:** Wika1979 (tl). **50 Dreamstime.com:** Arvind Balaraman (tc). **51 Dreamstime.com:** Poravute Siriphiroon (tc). **52 Alamy Stock Photo:** Morley Read (ca). **Dreamstime.com:** Slowmotiongli (crb). **53 Adobe Stock:** Miguel (bc). **Alamy Stock Photo:** imageBROKER.com GmbH & Co. KG / Arco / Therin-Weise (crb); Southeast Asia (clb). **Dreamstime.com:** Gstudioimagen (tl/x3). **54 Shutterstock.com:** Adilson Sochodolak

Cover images: *Front.* **123RF.com:** Wklzzz bl/ (Toco toucan); **Alamy Stock Photo:** Minden Pictures / Michael & Patricia Fogden cr/ (Butterfly), Wildlife GmbH crb; **Dorling Kindersley:** Peter Janzen cra, Oxford Scientific Films cla; **Dreamstime.com:** Leena Damle c/ (Cannonball Flower), Petlin Dmitry cla/ (Python), bc, Feathercollector clb, Isselee cb, Kira Kaplinski / Kkaplin ca/ (Flower), Pablo Hidalgo / Pxhidalgo bl, Slowmotiongli cl, Thawats ca, Evgeny Tkachev bc/ (Fish), Passakorn Umpornmaha tr, Ana Vasileva cr, Whiskybottle cra/ (Fungi); **Getty Images / iStock:** Atelopus cl/ (Pit Vipers), Yai112 tl; **Shutterstock.com:** Connect Images - Curated cr/ (Bananas), Dirk Ercken c, Milan Zygmunt tc; *Back:* **123RF.com:** Tim Hester crb; **Adobe Stock:** FotoRequest clb/ (Warbler); **Alamy Stock Photo:** Lophius bl; **Dreamstime.com:** 18042011e cr, Dirk Ercken bc, Marcouliana cla, Eka Jaya Permana clb, Wouter Tolenaars tr, Tr3gi br; **Getty Images / iStock:** Agus Fitriyanto tl; *Spine:* **Shutterstock.com:** Dirk Ercken